NEUROTIC WRITER: IS GREAT WRITER FREDDIE LEE SIRMANS SENIOR A TRUE GENIUS, OR JUST A PHONY ROCKING CHAIR THROWBACK NUT CASE?

NOTE: USA culture, culture, culture, you can't depend on the young being considerate and thankful when they have never been conditioned to be considerate and thankful, its all culture, baby.
F. L. SIRMANS LOG: 15 NOVEMBER 2017, 1210 HOURS.

GREAT WRITER FREDDIE LEE SIRMANS SENIOR IN ONE OF THOSE BLUE DOWN MOODS AND FEELING TOTALLY MISUNDERSTOOD, AIRS IT OUT
Folks, as a self-made writer I decided to do something I almost never do, do some soul searching and share my inner thoughts out loud. Making myself the issue to me is like wallowing in self-pity or being self-serving things I want no part of, but I make a very rare exception in this case.

The die was cast for me way back when I was being physical punished for wetting the bed as a young child, that punishment saddled me with an over powering neurotic pitiful look that still haunts me to this day.

No one can change the past, the wise thing to do is accept the hand you are dealt in life, learn to love and forgive then nothing can mentally destroy you.

In life and in my writing so many people see me as selfish, hard, and uncaring but nothing could be farther from the real truth, it's just that the will to survive is so strong in me.

No one can wade through the internal troubles, sorrows, and battles that I have experienced and keep a positive outlook without being spiritual to the core, being religious and spiritual is not necessarily the same thing.

Days To USA Economic Collapse 15 November 2017, 1825-0, 1824-0, 1823-0, 1822-0, 1821-0...

Destiny or fate chooses you; it is not the other way around. If I could just wish away my neurotic symptoms it would be a God send, but I can't, the morally weak and selfish sometimes takes the easy way out.

I am a firm believer that taking ones own life is the ultimate selfish act. A truly unselfish person that could care less what happens to himself/herself is not going to bring shame and pain down on a love one or family members, its just not going to happen.

There are many that would take the easy way out, but there are one or more human beings that they love too much to hurt in any way. Never mind me, my destiny is to survive and carry on my writing work. I know that my thinking and writing is out of phase with 95 percent of the USA population, still that doesn't prove me wrong.

Why do I continue to write and carry on? What fuels this urge and energy to write when so few reads my work? Finally, I have come to realize that it is my destiny to help save lives and my nation. Also, I believe there is no way without a purpose that I would still be walking this earth today without the protection of guardian angels.

Now I will shift gears, Government should never be a social and family provider, that role should be reserve for the nuclear family head of household, period. Government as a provider is like eating your seed corn, drinking your priming water, or eating your young. Western civilization cannot survive government being a family provider much longer.

Government as a family provider has all but destroyed the USA and Western Europe. Right now, here in the USA the focus is to seize more money in the form of taxes to feed the insatiable appetite of our welfare state beast. And to do that the money can only come directly or indirectly from the profits generated by American private businesses.

The #1 big problem is economic ignorance, before the "New deal" government as a free mass family provider never existed and was unheard of simply because it is dumb and leads to a dead end. And to put icing on the cake they enacted the arch-evil 1938 socialist minimum wage law too, duh.

Days To USA Economic Collapse 15 November 2017, 1825-0, 1824-0, 1823-0, 1822-0, 1821-0...

That really did it because that took all of the societal discipline out of our free market place economy, and stopped the boom and bust cycle from rotating. Sure, that was smart because everyone loves a boom cycle but hates the bust cycle and was happy the bust cycle was being staved off.

But, now guess what, with no bust cycle, culture rot and moral decay has had nearly eighty years to hollow out the inner fabric of USA culture and moral values with no resistance to counter balance nutty out of control liberalism. And right now, I have serious doubts the USA will be able to recover and survive, especially as a free nation.

Our USA culture and moral values are in almost total ruins and 95 percent of our population thinks the government owes them a living, which proves the old saying, "Ignorance is bliss", God help us. I would be surprised if USA business profits can feed the beast another five years without the USA economy totally collapsing, because everyday there are more mouths to be fed not less.

Here we are today with the inner fabric of our culture and moral values hollowed out and no one seems to care or give a damn. I put most of the blame on liberals and liberalism, but a lot of good men/women of sound judgment and good character stood silent while the country went to hell in a hand-basket.

Yet, we see government struggling with healthcare, taxes galore, and every other social and family provider issue under the sun while in the provider role, which government should never have been in, in the first place.

The solution to me is simple; the USA is not going to survive as a free nation if government continues as a social and family provider, period. I am just one lonely neurotic writer with an opinion, I have no power to decide anything, but that is just the way I see things.

I know it may seem hard and cold but to save our individual freedom and our nation in my view all that is necessary is to just repeal the insane arch-evil 1938 socialist minimum wage law, period. Sure, there will be a lot of pain and hardship, but the USA will survive as a proud independent free nation, otherwise the "Iron fist" awaits us all and no one knows where that will land us.

Days To USA Economic Collapse 15 November 2017, 1825-0, 1824-0, 1823-0, 1822-0, 1821-0...

When the 1938 minimum wage law is repealed, there shouldn't be any sudden changes; a genuine true free market place is all about discipline, balance, and control. A genuine true free market place operates on the boom and bust cycle that purges out all anti-survival extremes and nutty out of control liberal biases. And won't let any insane anti-survival extreme get out of hand.

A genuine true free market place economy is the only economic system known to man that will allow individual freedom and maintain an orderly disciplined society at the same time.

A genuine true free market place economy will never fail if government doesn't add wage and or price controls, because that will cripple and make weak every free market place economy. I still have serious doubts that the USA can recover from the severe destruction the 1938 minimum wage law has done to our culture and nuclear family foundation.

It is simply impossible for the USA government to continue in its current social and family provider role without soon totally collapsing the USA economy. Repealing the 1938 minimum wage law will relieve the government of its provider role, because that will end inflation, then people will be able to pay their own food and medical bills with money that has real buying power.

Otherwise to fail to repeal this arch-evil socialist law: It will be just a matter of time before the whole USA economy collapses, because the awesome financial load of the USA welfare state burden is becoming just too great, period.
FREDDIE LEE SIRMANS SR. LOG: UPDATED 12 NOVEMBER 2017, 2215 HOURS.

Days To USA Economic Collapse 15 November 2017, 1825-0, 1824-0, 1823-0, 1822-0, 1821-0...

LIKE A BROKEN RECORD: HERE WE GO AGAIN, WE KNOW THE LIBERALS ARE GOING TO BLAME THE GUN AS IF IT HAD A MIND OF ITS OWN.

There is almost nothing innate about a human being; all behavior is learned from somebody or something. If a child has never been conditioned to be responsible, accountable, and to show self-initiative he/she may grow up blaming all short comings on everybody but the man/woman in the mirror.

A healthy nuclear and extended family system foundation is a must to instill in the very young proper norms and traditions, period. And here I go again saying that the only thing that can save the USA is to "Repeal the insane arch-evil 1938 socialist minimum wage law".

Most people will wonder what the hell does the minimum wage law have to do with culture and public behavior? It has everything to do with culture and public behavior due to the extremely importance of societal discipline.

You see, a minimum wage law shuts down and kills the natural discipline power in a free market place economy. Only a genuine true free market place economy has the capacity to allow individual freedom and maintain an orderly society at the same time. Every other economic system demands an Iron fist to maintain an orderly society.

The USA and Western Europe never had any serious culture and moral problems until minimum wage laws and the welfare state came along. Sure, a minimum wage law may stave off the bust cycle and work fine in the beginning, but in about four generations it allows culture rot and moral decay to destroy everything even the foundation to rebuild upon.

To maintain an orderly society the law is extremely important, but the law alone can never control a free people with low morals and

Days To USA Economic Collapse 15 November 2017, 1825-0, 1824-0, 1823-0, 1822-0, 1821-0...

no respect for the law. Besides, the corrupt bias liberal news media only wants to punish conservatives for wrongdoings; otherwise they may look the other way.

In the end there are only two major ways to guarantee an orderly society: The Iron fist, or a genuine true free market place economy, period.

The republicans have had their chance to save the USA by repealing the arch-evil 1938 socialist minimum wage law. They have a Trifecta and control three branches of government, which is a miracle in itself.

But, I can tell you now I feel the republicans will be swept out in 2020 and the Dem's and liberals will come roaring back with a vengeance, and drive the final nail into our individual freedom coffin. Of course, I pray that I am completely wrong on this.

However, I understand the reason why my writing and books are almost totally ignored, there has not been enough real pain and suffering, yet.

The "Iron Fist" coming to the USA is now inevitable and closer than we think. And the only thing staving the Iron fist off right now is the 2nd amendment, which the liberals will find a way to deep-six when back in full power.

Folks, I write what I think and many times I am

wrong, but even a broken clock is right twice a day. Just chalk my writing up as food for though if nothing more.

Its simple, time and the future is on the side of the Dem's and liberals unless the insane arch-evil 1938 socialist minimum wage law is repealed, period. All because the republicans are failing to strike while the iron is hot.
                FREDDIE LEE SIRMANS SR. LOG: UPDATED 08 NOVEMBER 2017, 0924 HOURS.

Days To USA Economic Collapse 15 November 2017, 1825-0, 1824-0, 1823-0, 1822-0, 1821-0...

CAN THE USA SURVIVE BY GREAT WRITER FREDDIE LEE SIRMANS SR.?

I hate to say this, but I'm beginning to think the nutty bias liberal news media is making the USA ungovernable, and I believe they are out of touch with reality but fail to realize it, or maybe it is me that is out of touch with reality.

The USA is being engulfed and over run in numbers by liberals and liberalism due to the welfare state producing masses of them. Plus, the welfare state has turned this great nation into a lack of discipline soft p.... society with too many people having weak survival instincts.

Today people of good character and sound judgment is swimming against an over whelming tide of production-line liberalism that is impossible to overcome, there is just too many, even the poor is liberal and corrupt and killing in the womb by the millions today, which has never happened since the dawn of history.

All of this USA destruction results from a lack of societal discipline due to the enacting of the 1938 minimum wage law. And I believe beyond a shadow of doubt that the USA cannot be saved until that insane arch-evil 1938 socialist minimum wage law is repealed.
FREDDIE LEE SIRMANS SR. LOG: 31 OCTOBER 2017, 0247 HOURS.

FEDERAL INCOME TAX: WHY SHOULD THE POOR OR ANYONE NOT HAVE SKIN IN THE TAX PAYING GAME?

I, Freddie Lee Sirmans Sr. as a great writer have a big problem with the poor or anyone not paying any federal income tax, because that is what's wrong now, far too many people doesn't have any skin in the federal income tax game.

What's good for the goose is good for the gander, no one expects the very poor to pay more than 1 percent, which will be enough to give them skin in the game.

It is simple, just set the first bracket to start at $500 of income and everyone in that bracket pay 1 percent. And set the next higher bracket at $24,000 with a current normal percentage, and follow suit on up to the highest bracket.

Sure, 1 percent ain't much but with a 320 million population it's not chicken feed either, plus the poor won't be going along in this great country just for the ride.

Without paying any stake in federal income taxes why should those masses of hardcore liberal voters give a damn about the country or how high the tax rate goes. You can't bond with anything you're not invested in.

F. L. SIRMANS LOG: 29 OCTOBER 2017, 2115 HOURS.

Days To USA Economic Collapse 15 November 2017, 1825-0, 1824-0, 1823-0, 1822-0, 1821-0...

GREAT WRITER FREDDIE LEE SIRMANS SR. INJECTS HIS OPINION ON THE TRUMP SITUATION:

I see the endless search for wrong doing on the part of Trump by the nutty extreme liberal press and the liberal establishment. Sure, at times Trump may be raw and crude, but in this writer's view he is not a conniver or schemer that holds grudges. And you can like it or not he calls a spade a spade, period.

I believe Trump is a man that has seen the light and has been enlightened. The fact is when one fiercely and determinedly fights against great odds many times mighty unforeseen forces come to their aid.

There is a time and season for everything, and this writer believes the time was ripe for someone like Trump to come along to save the USA from all of this destructive nutty out of control liberalism.
SIRMANS LOG: 27 OCTOBER 2017, 1412 HOURS.

USA SURVIVAL WORDS TO THE WISE:
As a writer with great wisdom I believe Mother Nature with all of these natural disasters are forewarning the USA. Get rid of the 1938 minimum wage law, taking that action will get our economic house in order because the real big whammy mother of all disasters are on its way.

The days of a government social and family provider role are over, and have been over for the last twenty years. Going ever trillions of dollars deeper and deeper into debt is the only thing keeping the USA afloat. Government has no money in the first place, except what it takes from private business profit in form of taxes, directly or indirectly.

Get a grip USA; the people are supposed to finance a government not the government financing masses upon masses of individual citizens. That is the job reserve for the nuclear and extended family heads of household and the private sector.
FREDDIE LEE SIRMANS' LOG: 21 OCTOBER 2017, 1050 HOURS.

Days To USA Economic Collapse 15 November 2017, 1825-0, 1824-0, 1823-0, 1822-0, 1821-0...

BRIEF CURRENT EVENT INJECTION: FOOTBALL PLAYERS VERSUS TEAM OWNERS:

This writer sees the NFL situation like a parent being a buddy or pal to his/her child. The fact is sooner or later without a doubt the child is going to rebel; it's just a matter of time. The moral of the story is a parent should never be a buddy or pal to a child in the first place.

A child is not just a love item to be doted upon, a child is a separate individual that above all should be taught responsibility and accountability to stand alone on his/her own eighteen years later, period.

Old values and old norms evolved from years of tried and true proven survival experience. There is a proven reason why military officers are forbidden to fraternize with the enlisted. Free speech for all, baby.

There are only two major disciplines' to maintain an orderly society. Number one is the Iron fist, which has been used 99 percent of the time through out all history. And number two is a genuine true free market place economy, which uses the boom and bust cycle to purge out anti-survival threats.

What the USA has since the 1938 minimum wage law was enacted is a phony false weak p.... pretender of a true free market place economy. You can't have a true free market

17

place with a minimum wage law blocking wage freedom.

A minimum wage law blocks and kills the natural discipline power of a true free market place economy, which leaves our USA economy powerless to discipline and protect our society by not being able to purging out moral decay, culture rot, and aggressive extreme liberalism.
FREDDIE LEE SIRMANS SR. LOG: 12 OCTOBER 2017, 1439 HOURS.

Something gotta be done about all of this insane heinous killing of innocent, good, and decent people by self-serving nut cases. But, what must be done ain't what the liberals think should be done.

The hidden root and core problem what's causing all of this killing is the almost total destruction of the USA culture and moral foundation, which is due to generations of a welfare state. The welfare state has enabled liberalism to run amuck unchecked and is now totally out of control and running wild.

Days To USA Economic Collapse 15 November 2017, 1825-0, 1824-0, 1823-0, 1822-0, 1821-0...

The shallow minded weak survival instinct aggressive liberal news media mean well and have good intentions, but who was it that said the way to hell is paved with good intentions? We are at a point this writer feels only repealing the insane arch-evil 1938 socialist minimum wage law can save the USA. That is the only thing that can set free our hog-tied all mighty USA free market place economy.

Only a genuine true free market place economy has the discipline power to rein in out of control liberalism without destroying individual freedom in the process, like the iron fist. To God be the glory.

Starting with the Trump presidency the pendulum has swung. Finally out of control liberalism is being checked at the highest level. But, sadly it won't be nearly enough to rein in liberalism in terms of saving this great nation, his effort is like pissing on a barn fire expecting to put it out.

The only thing that can rein in self-destructive out of control run-away liberalism is to repeal our insane arch-evil 1938 socialist minimum wage law, period. Aggressive liberalism is the reason general public individual freedom is unheard of throughout human history.

Only the Iron fist has ruled throughout history. And the only way the USA pulled off this individual freedom thing is by the societal discipline of a true free market place economy, period. But, a good intention do-good liberal enacted our insane arch-evil 1938 socialist minimum wage law.

The most important thing about a true free market place economy is its discipline power. Well, a minimum wage law blocks and kills the discipline power in a free market place economy.

Days To USA Economic Collapse 15 November 2017, 1825-0, 1824-0, 1823-0, 1822-0, 1821-0...

So, with the enacted new 1938 minimum wage law that left the USA with a weak p.... economy and no institutional societal discipline to balance aggressive liberalism.

Conservatives tends to be strong on self-discipline, whereas liberals tend to be shallow thinkers and weak on self-discipline, but they are super aggressive. To maintain order there must be societal discipline and throughout history the iron fist tool was almost always used, but the Iron fist won't allow individual freedom.

The other effective tool that will maintain societal discipline plus embrace individual freedom at the same time is a genuine true free market place economy, which uses the cycles of boom and bust to purge out culture rot, moral decay, and every other extreme.

In other words freedom for all of the general public and especially individual freedom cannot exist very long without a genuine true free market place economy, liberalism will not allow it. Pick your poison USA; the Iron fist will definitely come to this great north American giant if our 1938 minimum wage law prevails and stay in place, period.
F. L. SIRMANS SR. LOG: 04 OCTOBER 2017, 0025 HOURS.

      USA ECONOMY: JUST THE FACTS MA'AM,
      AND NOTHING BUT THE FACTS MA'AM!

CURRENT EVENT INJECTION, LOOKING BACK:

I have fond memories of the two years I lived in Puerto Rico. At the time 1964-1966 I was a young U.S. Air Force Firefighter and fire and crash rescue man station at Ramey Air Force Base. The base was about 90 miles from San Juan and on the far western end of the island near the little town of Aguadilla.

While there I enjoyed some red beans and rice and fresh roasted pig along with the pleasant Caribbean climate. The paradise-like base has long since been closed. Just reminiscing and decided to share:

By writer, Freddie L Sirmans Sr. 01 October 2017, 1751 hours.

Days To USA Economic Collapse 15 November 2017, 1825-0, 1824-0, 1823-0, 1822-0, 1821-0...

Mother nature operates on laws and is infinitely wiser than human beings. The fact is the most important things in life one just can't see without a certain amount of hardship, struggle, or even suffering, which is also the only way deep, deep wisdom can be acquired.

Like the old Negro spiritual, "Nobody knows the trouble I've seen nobody knows my sorrow", many times the greatest struggles or suffering battles in ones life is internal and out of sight. That is why a seemingly normal person some times take their own life, all because they tried to fight an internal battle all alone without depending on the help of God or anyone else.

Another fact is the welfare state has made the USA a soft spoiled p.... society, and the only thing that can save us as a free nation is a genuine true free market place economy, perlod.

But, what is blocking the path to a genuine true free market place economy is the "Insane arch-evil 1938 socialist minimum wage law". The USA either repeals the 1938 minimum wage law or freedom perishes.

I see on TV about the government wanting to cut taxes and update the tax code. Well, anytime in this day and time when the government starts talking about improving the tax code I get nervous. The reason is both political parties want more revenue not less to support an ever-growing welfare state.

I'm one that believes that the only thing that is going to prevent the USA from a total economic collapse is for the federal government to get the hell out of the family provider business entirely, period.

Sure, I feel the government have a duty to help the very poor and needy to keep people from starving and freezing, but I believe the government should not give the citizens money to spend on an individual basis, the provider role must be reserve for the nuclear family head of household, period.

As a last resort after the nuclear and extended family system, church organizations, and community organizations is exhausted only then the government must provide or set up its own commissaries, clinics, and housing units for the very poor and needy. And above all use tokens or scrip for all who apply, that will protect the USA currency from being contaminated, inflated, and diluted like it is today.

But, the one step that must be done first before it is too late is: Repeal the insane arch-evil 1938 socialist minimum wage law. Otherwise, for the USA to continuing trying to feed the insatiable appetite of our monster welfare state beast is just plain dumb and stupid in this writer's view.

Days To USA Economic Collapse 15 November 2017, 1825-0, 1824-0, 1823-0, 1822-0, 1821-0...

Soon only crumbs will be left to finance our military or anything else. However, if the 1938 minimum wage law was repealed, an all powerful untied USA free market place economy would kick ass and do whatever it take to save this great nation.

The welfare state has split the USA into two main sometimes-hostile opposing camps. The two main camps are the Independent self-sufficiency minded

type and the dependent non self-sufficiency minded type.

The independent self-sufficiency minded type tends to be open minded and fear less about what other people and government thinks and more about what they are going to do for themselves. Whereas the dependent non self-sufficiency minded type tends to be just the opposite. And this camp also sees racism hiding behind every tree and even sees responsibility and accountability as racism.

In closing folks, I'm just one lonely self-made neurotic writer reaching out to touch the heartbeat of America; all I have is my opinion, that's all.
FREDDIE LEE SIRMANS SR LOG: 28 SEPTEMBER 2017, 1403 HOURS.

TRUMP VERSUS THE USA SPORTS WORLD!
The Trump versus USA sports world has got team owners between a rock and hard place. The fact is liberalism has taken over and dominates education and damn near every major institution in the USA. But, sports are one of the last bastions of strong moderate to conservative strongholds left in America.

Sure, the liberals are aggressive and makes a lot of noise but the real die hard sport's fans tends to be moderate to conservative. In the end I feel this whole issue will boil down to what the bottom line can take. In this writer's view the USA is in a complete moral and culture meltdown due to lack of societal discipline.

Old fashion norms and traditions are not being instilled in the very young by the head of households and respect for authority and other people's property is something from the past.

You can stop reading now because everyone by now should know what I see as the solution. If you are one of the few that don't know what I see as the solution: The answer is we must repeal the insane arch-evil 1938 socialist minimum wage law, that is the only thing that can untie and free the USA economy, which then will provide the necessary societal discipline to save us all.

Days To USA Economic Collapse 15 November 2017, 1825-0, 1824-0, 1823-0, 1822-0, 1821-0...

God, I ask in your name save my beloved homeland. Sure, taking the course of least resistance is almost always the easiest and p.... way out, but never forget there is no lasting enjoyment of anything in life without discipline, period. The greatness of a nation is determined by what it instills in its very young, the welfare state provider daddy has failed that task.
FREDDIE LEE SIRMANS SR. LOG: 24 SEPTEMBER 2017, 1342 HOURS.

SAVING THE USA ECONOMY BY FREDDIE LEE SIRMANS SR.
In this writer's view the secret of deep wisdom is beyond logic. Many conservatives still think the USA can budget cut its way out of an inevitable economic collapse, wrong. On the other hand the liberals are too shallow to see a need to cut spending as long as one taxpayer is left standing.

The liberals don't realize that every taxpayer gets his/her money to pay taxes directly or indirectly from the profits of some type of private business, period. Yet, many of them hate business, and are too shallow to know that profitable businesses are the golden eggs that make big government and the welfare state possible.

Well, I'm not educated and no genius but I feel I have raw wisdom above average. Sure, I am wrong on a lot of things but one thing I'm not wrong on is the USA economy is headed toward a total collapse. And depending on fine-tuning this and on the other hand fine-tuning that ain't gonna cut it, you know what President Nixon said about that, "He said he was going to hire him a one arm economist".

By political means the USA cannot be saved, but a genuine true free market place can even at this late stage. In my view the true solution is not new, I must have repeated it well over a thousand times but no one wants to hear it. "A thousand mile journal begins with the first step".

Days To USA Economic Collapse 15 November 2017, 1825-0, 1824-0, 1823-0, 1822-0, 1821-0...

The only way to get a genuine true free market place economy, which will save the USA is to first repeal our 1938 socialist minimum wage law, period; there is no other way. Everyone knows the free market place works and has withstood the test of time. I rest my case.

Nature's supreme law Of "Natural Selection" is based on a survival need, which means if there is no survival need for anything in nature it will slowly, start ceasing to exist. There must be a survival need for men and women to get married.

The welfare states in western civilization has made women independent to the point they no longer have a survival need for any man to survive. And it works both ways and is the reason there is more and more deadbeat dads. No sweat uncle sugar will take care of them, before the welfare state it was extremely rare for a man to leave his wife and kids totally stranded.

When you destroy the nuclear and extended family foundation you have nothing left in terms of human survival. It is no longer a matter of will the USA economy totally collapse, it is a matter of how much time we have left before it do collapse, period.
FREDDIE LEE SIRMANS LOG: 13 SEPTEMBER 2017, 1146 HOURS.

USA ECONOMY TEETERING ON THE BRINK OF A TOTAL COLLAPSE.
As a self-made writer with an exceptional strong survival instinct I decided to express my personal view concerning what's going down on the world stage. That said, I'm going to use a sports term often used especially in American football, "We need to get back to the basics".

We have gotten so far away from the basics that very few know what true basics are anymore. What is taught and instilled in the very young means everything in terms of maintaining a civil society. The first basic, which is the foundation for long tern human survival is maintaining a strong nuclear and extended family system, period.

The government seized the family provide role but it never taught or instilled proper norms and traditions in the very young. So, the big question now is how do we get back to the basics? The only way the USA is ever going to get back to basics and survive is to repeal the insane arch-evil 1938 socialist minimum wage law, period.

Days To USA Economic Collapse 15 November 2017, 1825-0, 1824-0, 1823-0, 1822-0, 1821-0...

I know the odds are 99 to 1 against that ever happening, but I can see that as the way out even if no one else can. In my view the USA economy is teetering on the brink of a total collapse and can't continue to be a social and family provider and have enough funds left to maintain a proper national defense, period.

Back to a strong nuclear and extended family system with the head of household as the provider is the only way the military will have enough funds to protect this great nation. When that is done the USA economy will have the capacity to take a punch from some pesky small country and counter punch with a total knockout.

Right now the USA economy has a glass jaw in this writers opinion. No government can carry the financial load of a social and family provider and survive very long. Practically all government income originates directly or indirectly from private business profit.

The only thing that can generate profit is a private business and the liberals through their shallow mindedness and crippling regulations is choking them almost to death.

All throughout history the family provider role has been reserved to the head of household until the "New Deal" came along. Then the government seizes the family provider role for itself and got drunk on power, and will never give up the role as long as a minimum wage law is in place.

Sure, everybody is so in love with FEMA and big government now, but what are you going to do when insane government spending has made money worthless and government can't play nursemaid anymore? Thank about it! It's going to happen! The insane arch-evil 1938 socialist minimum wage law must be repealed or else.
FREDDIE LEE SIRMANS LOG: 05 SEPTEMBER 2017, 0918 HOURS.

SURE RACISM EXIST IN THE USA BUT IT CAN'T HOLD A GOOD MAN/WOMAN DOWN

Days To USA Economic Collapse 15 November 2017, 1825-0, 1824-0, 1823-0, 1822-0, 1821-0...

In this writer's view the biggest problem in the USA today has nothing to do with race. I believe the biggest problem in the USA today is out of control run-away liberalism, which is due to a lack of individual responsibility and accountability.

Today most liberals can't tell the difference between individual responsibility, individual accountability, and racism. The responsibility and accountability of teaching our very young proper norms and traditions for the most part was lost when they enacted the 1938 socialist minimum wage law.

Now, after around four generations very few know what proper norms and traditions are. Today most shallow minded liberals believe if anyone stands up for individual responsibility and accountability they must be a racist, duh, the liberal Inmates is now running the asylum.

Sure, there is racism in America. And it always has and always will be racism in America to some degree as long as we have different races. But, with the almost unlimited amount of individual freedom we all have in America today no one with self-pride and an "I can do" attitude can be held down for long.

It is like winning ballgames in sports, the refereeing is a factor and sometimes they make bad calls, but true winners never focus and dwell on the negative. It is the same thing with racism, you don't focus and dwell on the negative, you move past it.

It is far more important on what one is going to do for him/her self than blaming the system and everything else under the sun in this imperfect world.

FREDDIE LEE SIRMANS LOG: 28 AUGUST 2017, 2205 HOURS.

THE U. S. SENATE FILIBUSTER RULE DAYS ARE NUMBERED!!!
Somebody needs to explain the facts about the role of the U. S. senate in terms of states rights. I wrote many years ago that the people gave up their real power when they allowed the government to seize the social and family provider role for its self.

Whoever is the provider is the real boss and has the final say like it or not. And on the other hand the states also gave up their real power by enacting the seventeenth amendment. Before the seventeenth amendment state governors and legislatures exercised almost total control over their two appointed senators.

Days To USA Economic Collapse 15 November 2017, 1825-0, 1824-0, 1823-0, 1822-0, 1821-0...

When senators were appointed they answered to their state governor and state legislature and didn't need to depend on special interest to get reelected. Sure, it was extremely political and bitter on who would be appointed, so the states took the course of least resistance and decided to let the people decide.

Constitutional-wise U. S. representatives were primarily designed to represent the people in congress, and U. S. senators were primarily designed to represent the states in congress. In this writer's view the senate filibuster rule days are numbered because if the republicans doesn't end it, when the Dem's get back in power they certainly will.

How in the hell can the states maintain a check on an all powerful out of control run-a-way big government when it can't control it's own two senators.

PS: No one truly knows, but this writer will take a shot in the dark and say: There is a better than 60 percent chance that the senate republicans will go over the 60 mark in 2018.
FREDDIE LEE SIRMANS LOG: 23 AUGUST 2017, 2353 HOURS.

THE WELFARE STATE HAS TURNED THE USA INTO A NATION OF NEGATIVE UNGRATEFULLY SELF-CENTERED IDIOTS, IJSMDH.

I have hired and provided jobs for people and know what it is like to struggle to make payroll when operating a business. How many of all of these self-righteous know-it-all people that ought to be counting their blessings ever sacrificed or done anything to help this nation survive.

We live in a nation with the most individual freedom and opportunity found anywhere on earth. Yet, we find hoards of people blaming any and everything under the sun but the real cause, which is the man/woman in the mirror for all of their shortcomings. If you won't do for yourself you haven't earned it and certainly don't deserve it, period.

Days To USA Economic Collapse 15 November 2017, 1825-0, 1824-0, 1823-0, 1822-0, 1821-0...

Sure, everyone sooner or later is going to need help from someone in life, but today far too many people don't really want a helping hand they want to be given a crutch to lean on for for the rest of their life.

Minimum wage laws and welfare states is what's destroying western culture, morals, and our nuclear family foundation, not terrorist or any other invading enemy. The 1938 USA minimum wage law must be repealed before it is too late.

The west is so internally corrupted it can't survive without immigration, period. The opioid problem alone speaks volumes, the military and manufacturing can't use people strung out on illegal mind-altering drugs.
F. L. SIRMANS LOG: 18 AUGUST 2017, 2155 HOURS.

GREAT WRITER FREDDIE L SIRMANS FEELS THE END OF THE USA MAY BE NEAR!!!
I have tried not to comment on all of this self-righteous and who may or may not be a racist. I love this country, but I also believe in constructive criticism.

I've said it before and will say it again; I don't think nothing is a bigger threat to the survival of the USA than the out of control liberalism that is running rampart today, not even a nuclear threat or anything else that I can imagine is more dangerous. The country is at the point of being ungovernable by anyone except a media placating weak big government sugar daddy liberal.

Extreme liberalism is out of control and running wild. The country is super high on emotionalism and true common sense and sound judgment is all but drowned out by political correction and racialism charges. We can forget about any bright future for the USA until extreme liberalism is reined in, period. If nothing else Trump is flushing out the political hypocrites and snakes that have been hiding their true color for years.

The only thing left that can possibly save the USA by breaking the liberalism death grip is to repeal the 1938 socialist minimum wage law. That act would untie the USA economy then the societal discipline from a true free market place would rein in all extremes. Otherwise, we might as well kiss this once great country good-by forever. Amen

F. L. SIRMANS LOG: 16 AUGUST 2017, 1748 HOURS.

Days To USA Economic Collapse 15 November 2017, 1825-0, 1824-0, 1823-0, 1822-0, 1821-0...

IT IS A SAD FACT THAT OVER 90 PERCENT OF THE AMERICAN PEOPLE CAN'T SEE THE DESTRUCTIVE POWER OF OUR MINIMUM WAGE LAW.

I, as a self-made crude neurotic writer have been drum beating on the destructive power of the USA arch-evil 1938 socialist minimum wage law for a long time, now. And it has been like beating my head up against a brick wall, which any normal writer would have long ago thrown in the towel.

I feel like the wood chopper, many times I have wished that I could just give up and walk away, but I feel it is my destiny to keep sounding the emergency distress call alarm to help save my beloved nation even if no one will listen. The main problem I face in getting anyone to see the logic of getting rid of the minimum wage law is perspective and wisdom to see the entire picture as a whole.

By the way the wood chopper after swinging his great axe many times to split a mighty oak block just tossed his axe aside and decided to give up and walk away feeling he had totally failed. He could not see any results but before walking away he decided to kneel down for a closer look and to his surprise he could see the beginning of a small split. The moral of the story is no positive human effort is a total waste.

Sometimes the right advice can change ones whole attitude, I remember when I was a young Airman in the military a Sgt. Williams said something that changed my whole attitude. I had become overly defensively and thinking I was getting too many raw deal. And one day I was bitching to Sgt. Williams and he said to me "Freddie you see all of these people around here, these people have eyes and if you are being mistreated everyone can see it". I got rid of my overly defensively attitude from that day on.

My high school basketball coach said something over sixty years ago that I have never forgotten, the team seemed too impatience to settle down and set up the plays properly, he said something obvious and very simple "The other team can't score when we have the ball". Well, in economic terms a merchant can't price the cost of his goods more than the poor and middle class can afford and still stay in business.

That is the rule and law on understanding basic free market place economic (meaning you can't get blood out of a turnip). And that law stands through hell and high waters unless government goes into competition against the working poor and middle class by giving cash to non-workers on an individual basis.

Days To USA Economic Collapse 15 November 2017, 1825-0, 1824-0, 1823-0, 1822-0, 1821-0...

In a true free market place economy the poor and middle class workers ability to pay is what sets the prices of goods, but when government pays non-workers on an individual basis that supplies enough guarantied customers so the merchant can say screw you working poor and middle class.

The government should stick with taking a small amount of profit for internal and external defense and the very few things the people can't do for themselves. That way the seller and the buyer will maintain a natural balance and prices can't get out of hand.

To protect the economy the government must never become a social and family provider unless it is going to provides its own commissaries, clinics, and housing units itself.

Anyway, so here we are making more and more inflated money that has less and less buying power. And even worse this whole process has all but totally destroyed our culture, moral standards, and our nuclear family foundation. As for the minimum wage law, none of this almost total destruction could have taken place without the full nelson choke hold it has on the USA free market place economy. Amen.
F. L. SIRMANS LOG: 13 AUGUST 2017, 2206 HOURS.

THE REAL QUESTION THAT MUST BE ASKED:
CAN THE USA GOVERNMENT PAY FOR AN ALL OUT WAR AND PAY FOR A WELFARE STATE AT THE SAME TIME?
The answer is a flat no! That is why it is so important to repeal "The arch-evil 1938 socialist minimum wage law" to first get the USA government out of the provider business if we are to survive, period. Trying to do both will quickly total collapse the whole USA economy without a doubt.

PS: In leadership when someone bucks the tide and suffers no consequence, then what is everyone complaining about???
F. L. SIRMANS LOG: 09 AUGUST 2017, 1009 HOURS.

CAN USA SURVIVE AND REBOUND FROM A TOTAL ECONOMIC COLLAPSE???

I want to ask the liberals and countless other shallow minded people that don't have the wisdom to pour piss out of a boot a very big question. Since you have unconditional blind faith in an omnipotent great father government, what are you going to do when the USA economy totally collapses and daddy government can't take care of you?

Days To USA Economic Collapse 15 November 2017, 1825-0, 1824-0, 1823-0, 1822-0, 1821-0...

The first thing is you won't get an answer because the question will be seen as hypothetical and something that could never happen. Well, I'm one that thinks it can happen but pray that it never will. However, if the USA doesn't a grip on getting back to a true free market place economy very soon it can and "Will" happen without a doubt in this writers view.

You won't get an answer to said question, so I will answer the question myself. Before the "New Deal" throughout history when a government went belly up the people relied on the strong nuclear and extended family foundation to regroup and get back on track. The boom and bust cycle is part of nature just like the life and death cycle, doctoring the economy can extend its life only so long but it must collapse or die at some point.

That is why I drum beat so hard and constantly on repealing the arch-evil 1938 socialist minimum wage law, which will untie the USA economy and restore our once strong nuclear and extended family foundation. I only want my beloved homeland the only home I know to be prepared to survive under all conditions; even knowing I will be hated like a mad dog for it.
F. L. SIRMANS LOG: 04 AUGUST 2017, 1322 HOURS.

THE CONSEQUENCE OF HYPOCRITICAL THINKING IN THE HEALTH CARE INDUSTRY IS HALF THE PROBLEM IN ITSELF

Believing in free health care is the same as believing in slavery, which is the only way to explain away the hard working people rendering the service.

The doctors, the nurses, and other support personnel have spent years of hard work and studying to achieve a high lever of proficiency. All of that said, the core problem in the USA health care industry is government involvement, period. Back before helpful do-good big government barged in there was never a problem with run-away prices, because market forces would never allow it.

Backs then the doctors were happy and the USA nuclear family structure was still strong, so if one family member were in desperate financial need the extended family would chip in. I will end by saying there is no logical reason why the medical profession shouldn't be able to list and advertise their prices the same as car dealers and other industries in this great free nation.

Listing and advertising prices alone would solve half of the problem in the USA health care industry. The USA is a free nation, make up your mind, what belongs to everyone, in a caretaker way belongs to no one.

Days To USA Economic Collapse 15 November 2017, 1825-0, 1824-0, 1823-0, 1822-0, 1821-0...

F. L. SIRMANS LOG: 02 AUGUST 2017, 1227 HOURS.

OBAMACARE COST WILL BE "THE STRAW THAT BROKE THE CAMEL'S BACK":

WHY WE HAVE AN OPIOID EPIDEMIC? USA NEEDS CONSTRUCTIVE CRITICISM, BECAUSE WE ARE "GOING TO HELL IN A HAND-BASKET" UNLESS WE GET A GRIP ON REALITY SOON.

In this writer's view the opioid epidemic is just another symptom of USA culture rot and moral decay due to liberalism. I wrote in an article recently "What good is it for a nation to gain power and riches but looses its soul and tradition".

Folks, I'm a writer with my own deep views, which very few can stomach. I feel the USA is living on its past glory and history, not on what liberalism is turning this great nation into. I see the liberals trying to turn the USA into a weak p.... feel good political correct socialist state.

Sure, love is one of the most important things in our entire human makeup. But, in terms of survival strength, power, discipline, and personal responsibility win the day, things liberals tend to downplay and dismiss to a fault.

When raising the young unconditional love that is not balanced with discipline in terms of survival can be one of the most dangerous things there is. No matter what problem exists there can be no lasting solution without discipline playing a role.

When the Arch-evil 1938 socialist minimum wage law was enacted, that killed the discipline in the USA economy. That was the thing that had maintains societal discipline through the whole nation. With that discipline gone the welfare state set about destroying the strong USA nuclear family system.

The main purpose for a nuclear and extended family system in the first place is to instill proper norms and traditions in the very young. That is the only thing that will safeguard and protect the future for any nation.

The biggest failure of the welfare state is no one is instilling and enforcing proper norms and traditions in the very young, especially the poor. Now, the parents don't really know what proper norms and traditions are. The USA can never be saved until that evil 1938 minimum wage law is repealed no matter what any one thinks.

Days To USA Economic Collapse 15 November 2017, 1825-0, 1824-0, 1823-0, 1822-0, 1821-0...

Only repealing that hog tying evil law can unbind the USA economy so it can get back its discipline power to rein in liberalism and save my beloved country, I'm willing to bet the farm on it.
F. L. SIRMANS LOG: 27 JULY 2017, 2236 HOURS.

REDUCING OR GETTING RID OF ENTITLEMENTS:
Everyone seems to be missing the point here, politically getting rid of entitlements is an impossible task, it can't be done, period.

The first thing is the liberals are too shallow to see their danger and is going to fight tooth and nails on keeping and getting even more entitlements. The only way to get rid of entitlements is to close the gate on what allowed them in, in the first place.

Before the "New Deal" the USA free market place economy would never have allowed entitlements to grow unabated. The problem is during the "New Deal" the USA free market place economy got hog-tied and afterward lacks the discipline to protect itself or the larger society.

The evil 1938 socialist minimum wage law has the USA economy in a full nelson where it is too weak to fight off entitlements, culture rot, moral decay, or anything else.

No political party or movement can get rid of entitlements, but an untied true free market place economy can and will if given the chance. Otherwise, the USA might as well accept its fate and be remembered as that once great land of the free and home of the brave.
F. L. SIRMANS LOG: 24 JULY 2017, 1510 HOURS.

(Great Writer and great thinker believes Trump is actually a liberal that has seen the light and has been enlightened to save this great nation from nutty out of control extreme liberalism, which is not humanly possible)

IF THE REPUBLICANS THINK THEY CAN EVEN CONSIDER MASS CUTS IN SOCIAL PROGRAMS AND STAY IN POWER, IJSMDH?
WRITER BELIEVES A TOTAL U.S. ECONOMY COLLAPSE IS IMMINENT:

Days To USA Economic Collapse 15 November 2017, 1825-0, 1824-0, 1823-0, 1822-0, 1821-0...

The duration of our USA welfare state is fast coming to an end, and in my view only the Republican Party will possibly save the USA from a bankrupted full socialist state with authoritarian rule.

As for the Dem's with their extreme shallow minded know-it-all liberal news media side-kicks riding shot gun they are lost somewhere out in fantasy land. And it is a lost cause to expect them to save the USA in terms of exercising financial responsibility.

The only way to prevent the USA from becoming a full socialist state and resorting to full authoritarian rule is to make a drastic structural change to the whole U.S. economic system.

Messing around with cutting social programs will only get the republicans booted out of power, and then the Dem's will have clear sailing right into a full socialist state. Once the Dem's and liberals get their socialist state and the mass civil disorder that follows, authoritarian rule will be inevitable.

This economy thing they call economic growth is a two headed snake in my view, it is maybe two parts inflation and maybe one part growth, what is correct, no one knows, I call the whole thing "Inbreeding".

A true free market place economy must be pure, which means very little government money should be injected into the private U.S. economy. Injecting mass amounts of government money into the private U.S. economy is like inbreeding in my view and is what causes inflationary phony growth.

Inbreeding contaminates the whole free market place economic process by destroying societal discipline throughout the whole society, which leads to the destruction of the nuclear family system.

Without a strong nuclear and extended family system almost no one teaches proper norms and tradition to the very young, then after four or five generations individual freedom is impossible. That is where the USA is at today, and the saddest part of all is so few has the wisdom and survival instinct to see past their nose to recognize a moral or physical threat staring them in the face.

Days To USA Economic Collapse 15 November 2017, 1825-0, 1824-0, 1823-0, 1822-0, 1821-0...

The only thing that is going to save the USA is to separate the private U.S. economy from being deluged by the injection of mass tons of government money. By stopping that deluged it will solve the U.S. health care problem, the U.S. immigration problem, the lack of jobs problem, and all other dire problems wrecking havoc on our beloved country, a genuine true free market place economy never fails.

As to the solution to save our free nation: "There is more than one way to skin a cat", In my view the arch-evil 1938 socialist minimum wage law has the USA economy in a full nelson in terms of our economy being a free market economy.

One way to set the USA economy free and save our freedom is starve the welfare state beast by simply repealing the 1938 minimum wage law. Another way is to prevent government money on an individual basis from being injected into the private USA economy and contaminating it to no end.

Almost everyone agree that the federal government has a responsibility to help the poor and needy, but the problem is when government money is given out on an individual basis that competes directly against the poor hard working citizens thereby driving consumer prices beyond their reach.

The only way to protect the working poor and middle class in the private U.S. economy and government still help the poor and needy is for government to provide its own hospitals, commissaries, and housing units. And above all tokens or script must be used for all who qualify, that way the working poor and middle class in the private sector will be protected and be able to pay their own food and hospital bills out of pocket like before the welfare state came about with the "New Deal".

There is no need for the government to get directly into the nut and bolts of daily operations, the whole process can be contracted out, because the whole focus is to protect the working poor and middle class in the private economy from living from pay check to pay check like it is now.

Days To USA Economic Collapse 15 November 2017, 1825-0, 1824-0, 1823-0, 1822-0, 1821-0...

Folks, that is the way I see it, I'm just one man with some strong political views, I realize very few will agree with me on anything. My only goal is in my own way help save my beloved country for my grand kids and on down the line.

I know many of my views may seem hard and cold and even to the extreme. Maybe some people need waking up. And I must say that I am deeply thankful that I can still freely write what I think and feel without disappearing in the middle of the night.

God, save my beloved USA. And God, I thank you in advance for saving my beloved country. Amen.

POST STATEMENT:
You can't have a strong nuclear and extended family system and a well-established welfare state at the same time. If the USA had a strong nuclear and extended family system it could survive a total economic collapse and quickly regroup and rebuild. But, as it is now if the USA economy totally collapsed with millions upon millions solely dependent on government, less than half of our 321 million population might not survive a total economic collapse.

Unless the USA welfare state is abandoned soon a total economic collapse is imminent in this writer's view. Sure, not only the shallow minded liberals can't conceive of this being possible, but due to the conditioning of our welfare state 90 percent of the whole country can't either. World economy help would only buy little time.

In fact the U.S. economy is still the main engine driving the world economy, so if the U.S. economy goes down the world economy goes down with it also in my view. I pray that my wild imagination is just that, phew.

One thing that I am sure of is, if the republicans don't get rid of the filibuster the Dem's will when they get back in control. Hell, the liberals no longer even honor a peaceful change of power

Days To USA Economic Collapse 15 November 2017, 1825-0, 1824-0, 1823-0, 1822-0, 1821-0...

anymore; the shallow minded know-it-all liberal news media mentally still have not accepted the Trump presidency.
F. L. SIRMANS SR. LOG: 25 MAY 2017, 1810 HOURS.

A BEGINNING OF THE END TO A FREE USA: THE SHALLOW MINDED KNOW-IT-ALL LIBERAL NEWS MEDIA HAS GROWN JUST TOO POWERFUL

Never forget, Americans of good character and sound judgment has eyes and ears and can see for themselves what is going on. That said: With all of the political hoopla going down with the shallow minded know-it-all liberal news media flexing their raw muscle power, I wouldn't be one bit surprised if a huge nation saving backlash occurred at the polls.

This writer believes liberalism is totally out of control in the USA and only repealing the U.S. 1938 minimum wage fair labor law can stop them from totally destroying this great nation. There is almost no societal discipline left in the USA anymore, which means some form of authoritarian rule, is inevitable, period.

I am totally convinced that liberalism is out of control and is going to destroy my beloved homeland unless it is brought under control, and nothing is going to convince me otherwise, period. You see, the shallow minded know-it-all liberal news media is a micro cosmos of nearly half of the entire USA. And that is due to our liberal induced welfare state.

The biggest failure of all from our welfare state is almost no one is teaching and enforcing proper norms and traditions in our very young. So, after more or less 80 years to some degree

Days To USA Economic Collapse 15 November 2017, 1825-0, 1824-0, 1823-0, 1822-0, 1821-0...

95 percent of the USA population has weak survival instincts and can't see past their noses. And as far as any real societal discipline, that is something from the distant past.

Only repealing our 1938 minimum wage law can give the USA back a true free market place economy. Then an untied true free market place economy will supply the necessary societal discipline to rein in liberalism and save our great nation. Otherwise, authoritarian rule is inevitable, and after that our individual freedom will be lost forever, period.
F. L. SIRMANS SR. LOG: 18 MAY 2017, 1219 HOURS.

GREAT WRITER F. L. SIRMANS SR SEES A WAY TO ESCAPE THE OBAMACARE TAR BABY

When using government money, the main focus for using tokens or script is to keep that money on an individual basis from competing and driving up consumer prices in the private U.S. national economy.

The government could provide its own hospitals for those that can't afford to purchase private health insurance. That is the only thing that is going to save the republicans from the tidal wave of socialize medicine coming at them. There is no reason for government to get into the nuts and bolts and daily operations, the whole process could be contracted out.

Writer feels the pillar for the whole thing is tokens or script must be used by all qualifying patients, otherwise it would be just another big government march deeper into socialism.

Days To USA Economic Collapse 15 November 2017, 1825-0, 1824-0, 1823-0, 1822-0, 1821-0...

Any script method that can be used in the private sector economy will defeat the whole purpose; it must be limited to government set-aside facilities only, period.
F. L. SIRMANS SR LOG: 11 MAY 2017, 1036 HOURS.

PS: Just like back during the 2016 election the Know-it-all shallow minded anti-survival liberal news media propaganda noise machine is firing on all cylinders at full throttle. God, help us again. Amen.

The know-it-all shallow minded liberal news media is trying to whip the political correction hoards into an uproar like an out of control screaming hysterical individual that only a hard slap can bring back to sanity. God, save our beloved nation from educated liberal fools. USA free press gone amuck! Child please?

WRITER F. L. SIRMANS SR. GETS FED UP AND DECIDES TO GIVE THIS LECTURE ON OBAMACARE

The reason this writer believes the Obamacare time bomb cannot be defused and is going to soon blow the U.S. economy out of the water, is because of flawed modern U.S. economic thinking.

Except for the shallow minded liberals I think almost everyone with even an ounce of common sense and sound judgment knows the U.S. economy is headed toward a total collapse unless spending is brought under control. The problem is the great thinkers, the think tanks, and the powers that be really doesn't have a clue as to how to slow down or stop this suicide spending train to hell.

If the liberals had their way they would make Obamacare a one-payer system tomorrow. And follow that up by turning the whole country into a failed socialist state like Venezuela. The republicans are now in control of all three branches of government, but is caught between a rock and a hard place simply because they want their cake and want to eat it at the same time.

I will now shift gears: In this writer's mind solving the Obamacare riddle for me is a piece of cake if one knows what to do, otherwise it is definitely going to soon sink the whole U.S.

Days To USA Economic Collapse 15 November 2017, 1825-0, 1824-0, 1823-0, 1822-0, 1821-0...

economy. I have said many times that as a self-made writer I believe I can visualize and dissect an economy as well as anyone.

I believe before one can truly understand the U.S. economy one must first understand what a true free market place economy is. I don't know what the U.S. economy really is, but it is not a true free market place economy, it is some kind of welfare state hybrid system in my view.

Government and it's spending is one thing, and the private free market place economy is another thing. And one thing I know is they are two things of a different color and should never be mixed or blended if a free nation is to survive long term. Practically all government income and wealth originates from some form of private business "Profit", period.

A true free market place with unrestricted competition will generate far more profit than any other economic system known to man. Before government the early societies had a free market place with unrestricted competition generating tons of profit, but what is going to stop the meanest, baddest, and strongest from taking what others earned, some form of government was a must as a protector and enforcer for a society to exist.

The primary purpose for government is to first protect the nation internal and external. Fast forward to today in the year of 2017 with government taking in trillions of dollars directly or indirectly from the profit of private American businesses.

Government can spend that money any way it see fit even helping the people and it won't damage the golden goose that lays the profit egg, except one way the government should never spend that money if a nation is to survive long term. That one way what the government must never do is give cash or it's equivalent to individual citizens on an individual basis, period.

If a free government does that its survival time there after is a hundred years more or less, unless that mistake is corrected. Once a government does that government money competes on an individual basis directly against the hard working citizens in the private sector.

That causes consumer inflation and prevents the free market place from maintaining discipline and order through out the society. Then with almost no market place societal discipline the first casualty is a lack of respect for authority, followed by almost no one teaching and instilling in the very young proper norms and traditions, and finally, if it feels good do it, and as to the safety and protection of our future unborn generation, let them be damned.

I will begin closing this down by saying: Anytime government feels a need to help the poor and needy on an individual basis it must do the

Days To USA Economic Collapse 15 November 2017, 1825-0, 1824-0, 1823-0, 1822-0, 1821-0...

providing itself by providing the hospitals, commissaries, and housing units, and using token or script to prevent government dollars from competing against hard working citizens in the private sector free market place. Otherwise, the **$20,000,000,000,000** and growing deficit is going to do us in if moral decay and culture rot doesn't get us first.

The only way I can see for the republican to solve the Obamacare health care problem is to set up its own government run hospitals for all that can't afford to purchase private care insurance. And the kicker is, if government gets the hell out of private health care completely the consumer price for health insurance will drop like a rock.
F. L. SIRMANS SR. LOG: 09 MAY 2017, 1819 HOURS.

THE END

WEBSITE: FLSirmans.com

I'm Throwing in a little fable I wrote many years ago, I hope you enjoy it.

Chapter 1

Once upon a time there was a little town called Health-land kingdom, located right off the big super MD highway leading to the great cure-all metropolis. In this town lived vitamins, minerals, herbs, humans, and other nutrients.

The town's main goal was to keep all of its citizens healthy because anyone that they failed to keep healthy would have to face terrible traffic jams on the super MD highway leading to the great cure-all metropolis.

Jim-Niacin (vitamin B-3). Jim-Niacin doesn't stand alone; he is a member of the very powerful B vitamin family. In Health-land Jim-Niacin's job is essential to promote life and good health. He regulates the metabolism and assists in other body processes, even though he is needed in small amounts compared to proteins and carbohydrates. As a coenzyme Jim-Niacin works to make sure the human body functions as it should. There are two major types of vitamins: the water soluble and the oil soluble. Jim-Niacin belongs to the water-soluble type vitamins, therefore his doses must be replaced everyday because the human body doesn't store his doses like the oil soluble type.

Since Jim-Niacin is only one member of the very powerful B vitamin family he shouldn't work alone; he should be balanced with other B vitamin members. Jim-Niacin is not a bad or evil fellow, but he does have a bad reputation.

Humans are afraid of Jim-Niacin and rightly so because in too high doses he may damage the liver, or in too low doses he does no good. But, that is not the only reason human fear Jim-Niacin. Jim-Niacin deals with circulation and the skin, and he will heat the skin up like it is on fire and turn it as red as a beet.

When this happens to a human for the first time, it will scare some humans half to death, but don't be put off, the flushing of the skin is normal when dealing with Jim-Niacin. It's not pretty or pleasant but that is how Jim-Niacin unclogs the capillaries and small blood vessels throughout the body.

Captain Fredrico (human). Orry Fredrico is one of many humans that Was born and raised in Health-land Kingdom. Orry Fredrico is a Carpenter by trade, but as long as he Could remember he loved the sea. As a small child he would stand by The ocean for hours just staring out to Sea.
As a teenager he would try to Hop aboard any boat going salt water Fishing. During his senior year in high School he went on one of those deep Sea fishing cruises that goes out for Four or five hours at a time. On this Cruises he met Jan Flemmings. Jan Also loved the sea and they instantly

Days To USA Economic Collapse 15 November 2017, 1825-0, 1824-0, 1823-0, 1822-0, 1821-0...

Became attracted to each other. Within days Jim started dating Jan.

VC (vitamin C). VC also belongs To the water-soluble type of vitamin. VC is truly a heavyweight among Vitamins. VC is known as a very Power antioxidant. He is a mighty Human body protector. He protects the human body against harmful effects of pollution. He helps to prevent cancer. He helps to lower cholesterol and other protection functions.

Scurvy is a disease that moves in when there is a deficiency in vitamin C protection. Years ago, passengers on ships on long voyages without fresh fruits and vegetables had a problem dealing with scurvy.

Jan Flemmings (human). Jan is a Health-land Kingdom toy soldier's brat. Just like Captain

Fredrico she has always loved the sea. She was mostly unanchored until she met her soul mate Orry Fredrico. At first she thought he loved the sea too much and would not be a good provider, but his dreamy bedroom eyes soon won her over.

      VE (vitamin E). VE belongs to the oil soluble type of vitamin. VE is another mighty antioxidant. VE is very important in fighting cancer and cardiovascular disease. Vitamin E is a giant in so many ways. VE is a natural blood thinner. He promotes good blood circulation, he promotes healthy skin, healthy hair, and so many other healthy body functions. Vitamin E actually belongs to a family of eight but falls into two major groups. These two groups are tocopherols and tocotrienols. It is the alpha-tocopherols form that is the most potent. That is the group VE belongs to.

Days To USA Economic Collapse 15 November 2017, 1825-0, 1824-0, 1823-0, 1822-0, 1821-0...

John-Pyridoxine (vitamin B-6). John-Pyridoxine like his cousin Jim-Niacin is a member of the very powerful B vitamin family. The fact is John-Pyridoxine is involved in more bodily functions than any other single nutrient. John-Pyridoxine deals with both the mental and physical health.

He deals with water retention, sodium and potassium balance, and fights hard against allergies, arthritis, asthma, carpal tunnel syndrome, and on and on. Just like his cousin Jim-Niacin, John-Pyridoxine shouldn't fight alone; he should be balanced with other members of the mighty B vitamin family.

Mister Disease. Mister and his family showed up one day in Health-land Kingdom. No one seems to know where he came from. All anyone knows is he is mean and evil. He has no friends and is known to attack humans sometimes without provocation.

He has no conscience and will attack anyone that is weak and helpless. The town and kingdom has tried to keep him out, but somehow he always sneaks back in. Our vitamins, minerals, herbs and others nutrient citizens have done a good job fighting him off, but Mister Disease is a very, very tough customer.

     Jim-Niacin and the other nutrient protectors of Health-land Kingdom were joyfully patting themselves on the back because they were doing a good job protecting the city's population from Mister Disease and his cohorts. Jim-Niacin decided to telephone his cousin John-Pyridoxine. Jim could hear the phone making its fourth ring.

"Hello," said John-Pyridoxine.
" This is Jim-Niacin, I decided to give you a call and touch base on a

matter that I've been tossing around in my mind lately."
"Tell me about it," said John-Pyridoxine.

"Well, I've been thinking that all of the vitamins, minerals, humans, herbs, and other nutrient citizens should get together and have a big town hall meeting. What do you think."

"I think it is a very good idea," said john-Pyridoxine.
" Good, then it's a go, I'm going to start right away making plans," said Jim-Niacin. "John you take care now, I'll talk to you later."
" Bye," said John-Pyridoxine.

Chapter 2

    Orry Fredrico and Jan Flemmings got married after a one

year engagement. Orry got an associate degree in carpentry from the local technical college. Twenty five years later Orry and Jan are now the parents of a seventeen-year-old son Rob, and a fifteen-year-old daughter Melinda.

Almost everyone calls Orry   by his nickname Captain Fredrico after he bought his first boat about fifteen years ago. The boat was a fourteen footer with a big Mercury motor. Captain Fredrico now operates his own contracting business.

It is almost six o'clock p.m. when Captain Fredrico lets himself in the carport door which opens directly into the kitchen. He found his wife Jan bending over checking her meat loaf in the oven.

"Hello dear," said Captain Fredrico in a somewhat tired voice.
" Hello Orry, how did your day
" Pretty good, but my right wrist that's been bothering me the last couple of weeks seems to be getting

worse, especially at night after I fall asleep. Sometimes I wake up with a numb tingling in my right hand. It feels like somebody is sticking pins in my hands."

"Orry, I think you need to check with one of the vitamin citizens. That sounds like something John-pyridoxine might be able to help you with."

"I think you are right dear, I will give him a call in a few days.

After Marrying Orry, Jan Fredrico decided to postpone a career of her own. Becoming a full time housewife and mother was very fulfilling to Jan. She even took on the awesome job of home schooling her kids.

VC (vitamin c) enjoys his job in Health-land Kingdom taking care of its citizens. He has a very good reputation. Humans were using him probably more than any other vitamin. Being one of the most powerful antioxidants, he was in great demand these days.

In fact, he was being used to fortify many of today's foods. He thought the town hall meeting was a great idea. Why didn't he think of it? The vitamins and other nutrients were doing a good job fighting off Mister Disease, but he knew that they couldn't let their guards down, ever.

Just like VC, VE (vitamin E) is another very powerful antioxidant but of the oil soluble type. VE is probably in even greater demand these days than VC. With so many humans becoming diabetics these days, VE with his natural blood thinning power is a real workhorse. VE is also looking forward to the big town hall meeting coming up soon.

Days To USA Economic Collapse 15 November 2017, 1825-0, 1824-0, 1823-0, 1822-0, 1821-0...

On this Monday morning John-Pyridoxine was kicking back at his office when the phone ring.
" Hello," said John-Pyridoxine.
" May I speak to John-Pyridoxine?" said the voice on the line.

"This is he," said John-Pyridoxine.
" I'm Captain Fredrico and I've been told you may be able to help me concerning an ailment. I believe I have a case of carpal tunnel syndrome."

"You have the right vitamin, that is one of my many areas of expertise."
" Then you will be able to help me," said Captain Fredrico.

"Hold on a minute, I didn't say that. Let me explain the situation here, then I can tell you what I may be able to do. Listen Captain, I'm going to explain what I do, and it should take care of your problem, but then it may not. If I can't cure it, then

75

I recommend you take the super MD highway to the cure all metropolis."

"I understand," said Captain Fredrico.
" Now, first off," said John-Pyridoxine, "my maximum dose is 300 mg. per day, that way I will not damage any nerves. In most cases 100 mg. of my dose will cure the problem. The golden rule with taking any nutrients is don't take more than the recommended dose, because too much of anything may cause damage, and never take nutrients on an empty stomach. So, Captain if you understood everything I said, come by as soon as possible. We have a walk in policy."

"Thank you sir, I should be there within the hour."

Mister Disease is very upset with himself for being unable to do more damage in Health-land Kingdom. He

Days To USA Economic Collapse 15 November 2017, 1825-0, 1824-0, 1823-0, 1822-0, 1821-0...

feels he should be able to bring in more of his friends like cancer, AIDS, and even some of his very old friends like the black plague.

He was getting fed up with those damn vitamins, minerals, herbs, and other nutrients. The thing about those nutrients is they are keeping him from getting a foothold in Healthland Kingdom. He feels that if he could just get a foothold he would be able to start an epidemic.

Mister Disease decided that he would just have to work harder. Sooner or later those humans are going to think that they are safe and slack up on utilizing the nutrients. That is the time he plans to throw his best punch. He feels that if his friend AIDS just keeps up the pressure, he has the best shot at causing an epidemic.

Most humans don't know Jim-Niacin and many of those that do

tend to fear and avoid him. As one of the smallest members of the powerful B vitamin family, being unknown is about to change. The reason is Jim-Niacin along with his cousin John-Pyridoxine are the ones that called for and organized the town hall meeting coming up in a few weeks. The whole thing was originally Jim-Niacin's idea.

Since then Jim has invited the town fathers and secured all of the permits needed to stage such an event. Jim has contacted other town nutrients and humans, many of them had never heard of him, or knew who he was.

Chapter 3

Captain Fredrico had lived in Health-land Kingdom all of his life and he loved this town. Captain Fredrico got an invitation from Jim-Niacin to attend the town hall meeting coming up in a few weeks.

Captain Fredrico had heard the name Jim-Niacin before and even knew he was a member of the mighty B vitamin family, but that was about all he knew about Jim-Niacin. He didn't know what kind of work or anything else Jim-Niacin did.

Captain Fredrico had heard that the vitamins and other nutrients citizens had become concerned about the health of Health-land Kingdom. The main work our nutrient citizens do is protect our human population from characters like Mister Disease and his friends.

The nutrients knew that cancer and AIDS had almost destroyed a few other towns in the Kingdom. The town hall meeting got Captain Fredrico to thinking. The mayoral election will be coming up in about a year. Captain Fredrico decided that he was going to throw his hat in the ring. Of course he would have to talk it over with his wife Jan first.

After putting in a hard day's work, on his drive home Captain Fredrico thought about the pesky dry skin that had been plaguing him for years. It has slowly become more and more of a problem as time past.

Now it has become a real nuisance. It has come to the point that he has to lotion down almost his whole body every time he takes a shower.
He feels that is unmanly, only women like to lotion their bodies. He has tried everything, but to no avail.

He had even got on the crowded super MD highway and went to the cure all metropolis, but still to no avail. At the cure all metropolis all they did was to prescribe an extremely expensive body cream that did little better than over the counter creams.

He felt truly at his wits end.
There didn't seem to be any hope, he

Days To USA Economic Collapse 15 November 2017, 1825-0, 1824-0, 1823-0, 1822-0, 1821-0...

would just have to accept his miserable fate. As Captain Fredrico let himself in the carport door, Jan was making a salad.
" Hello, dear," said the Captain in a husky sexy voice.

"Hello, sweetheart," said Jan in a wooing voice as she dropped everything and rushed over and planted a seductive kiss on her husband's left cheek.

"Now, you go ahead and clean up, dinner will be ready in a few minutes. By the way Rob complained about a bout of indigestion after lunch."

"Did you check with Mr. Blue Page?" said the Captain.
" Yes, he gave me the names of several nutrients that work in that area. The two nutrients that I decided to use were Stewart-Ginger Root and Henry-Acidolphilus. Each one of them gave me heavy doses to give Rob as needed."

"Good, now let me go ahead and wash up, then you can tell me all about it later." After the Captain and all of the family had sat down to dinner and the blessing was said, the Captain revisited the subject of Rob's indigestion.

"How is your stomach feeling now, Rob," said the Captain.
" It's fine now, dad, since Mom had a couple of the nutrients treat it."
" I wasn't sure what to do until after my talk with Mr. Blue Page," said Jan.

"Mr. Blue Page gave me the names of several nutrients that work in the area of indigestion. These are the names that Mr. Blue Page gave me that deal with indigestion: Stewart-Ginger Root, Calvin-Fenugreek, Bonnie-Papaya, Henry-Acidophilus, and Sammy-Oat bran tablets.

He also stressed that they did their work with either tablets or capsules."

Days To USA Economic Collapse 15 November 2017, 1825-0, 1824-0, 1823-0, 1822-0, 1821-0...

"Excuse me for changing the subject, I have a very important announcement to make," said the captain.

"Jan, the mayoral election is coming up in about a year and I would like to know if you have any objections to me throwing my hat into the ring."

"Gee, I don't know? I've never thought about being a politician's wife. Do you think you can win?"
"Dad, I love it, I think it is a great idea," said Melinda.
"Me too," said Rob.

"I can't guarantee you I will win, but I believe if I get out there and shake enough hands I'll have a very good shot."
" Dad, I'll campaign for you," said Melinda.

"Honey, If you really want to run, then count me in as your number one supporter," said Jan.

"Then it's all settled You are looking at the next mayor of Health-land Kingdom."

Ever since John-Pyridoxine had agreed to help his cousin Jim-Niacin organize the big town hall meeting coming up soon, he had stayed busy calling and talking to the citizens of Health-land Kingdom.

Chapter 4

Mr. Disease was aware of the big town hall meeting coming up in a few days, and he definitely was not pleased about what he was hearing. The word was they were going to try to get rid of him. Mr. Disease was not going to let that deter him, that had been tried before with his ancestors all throughout history.

Sure, the discovery of DDT, penicillin, and modern antibiotics had given his family some big setbacks, but some of his old friends like tuberculosis were beginning to make a comeback, and the new kid on the block, AIDS, was really beginning to raise hell.

Mr. Disease felt that as far as he was concerned, let them have all of the town hall meetings they want to, it was not going to put him out of business.

Mr. Disease watches the super MD highway often and as far as he could tell it was becoming even more crowded each day. Even at the big super cure all metropolis they haven't been able to get rid of his best friend Mr. Cancer. Mr. Cancer is still doing an awful lot of damage.

On this Monday morning Jan Fredrico sure didn't want to battle the traffic jams on the super MD highway going to the cure all metropolis. It was just one of those days, Her daughter was down with a cold and she herself was dealing with a slight kidney infection.

She didn't know? Maybe it was something she ate that was causing her back a slight ache in the area of her kidney. She knew that it would save her a lot of money and time if she called Mr. Blue Page and found out which vitamins, minerals, herbs, or other nutrients that specialized in the areas of their ailments.

Jan decided to give the nutrients twenty-four hours to do their work, then if there was no obvious improvement she would get on the crowded super MD highway to the cure all metropolis. Jan dialed Mr. Blue Page. The voice on the line said, " You have reached Mr. Blue Page directory."
"Mr. Blue Page, this is Jan Fredrico.   My daughter has a cold and my kidneys have a slight ache. I would like for you to give me the names of the nutrients that specialize in the areas of our illness."

"Very well, madam. In the area of the   kidneys, the association of

Days To USA Economic Collapse 15 November 2017, 1825-0, 1824-0, 1823-0, 1822-0, 1821-0...

VC and Cranberry handle that, and in the area of colds and flu, the association of Garlic, Echinacea, and Golden Seal handle that. Will that be all, madam?"

"Yes sir, and thank you very much," said Jan. Taking advantage of their-walk in policy, Jan didn't have to wait long before she was able to see VC, the very powerful vitamin C antioxidant.

"Mrs. Fredrico," said VC, " We give our doses in mostly tablet form. I am of the water soluble type, the body does not store my doses. Taking too much of my dose is washed out with the urine. But, taking too much of my dose also may cause diarrhea or stomach soreness in some humans.

Rule number one for dealing with your kidney problem is to keep drinking lots of water, then take 2000 mg. of vitamin C tablets three or four times a day after a meal, also take 2000 mg. of cranberry fruit capsules three of four times a day after a meal. That should take care of your problem, Mrs. Fredrico."

Jan next proceeded to take her daughter by the association of Garlic, Echinacea, and Golden Seal to take care of her cold. After a short wait Jan and her daughter were lead in to see Hannah-Garlic.

Hannah-Garlic came from one of the most powerful and popular of all herb families. Even the Roman army would not go into battle without a member of the garlic family coming along.

Hannah-Garlic instructed Jan to give Melinda throat lozenges if needed, then give her a dose of about 1400 mg. of odor controlled garlic, three or four times a day after a meal, also give her a 1500 mg. dose of combination echinacea-golden seal three or four times a day after a meal.

"You should see some obvious improvement in twenty four hours; if not take the super MD highway to the cure all metropolis.

"It is also helpful to take heavy doses of vitamin C after a meal at the beginning of a cold. But, only at the beginning of a cold, because if congestion sets in, vitamin C tends to make it worse. Warning: Never take vitamin C or others nutrients on an empty stomach," she said.
After thoroughly going over everything, Hannah-Garlic said, " That is it, Mrs. Fredrico, do you understand all of my instructions?"

"Yes, Herb Garlic and thank you very much." While driving home Jan reminded herself to do her neck exercises when she got home. It has been quite awhile since stress has caused her neck to tense up, but she Decided that she would go ahead and do the exercises anyway.

Jan believed that feeling stress is a normal part of life. The better one learns how to deal with life's frustrations the better one will be able to cope with stress. Stress affects people in many different ways. It may affect some in physical ways such as headaches, neck aches, shoulder aches, etc.

To deal with physical aches it is helpful to do these exercises. These exercises are done sitting on the side of the bed. Sit on the side of the bed with feet apart flat on the floor for balance. With both hands rolled into a fist, place them thumbs inward down on the bed several inches from the body on each side.

Start the first exercise by twisting the neck and entire upper body counter-clockwise as far as possible, then twist the neck and entire upper body clockwise as far as possible. Do these exercises in sets of one hundred as many times as one desires.

Start the second exercise by leaning the head as far as possible on the right shoulder, then lean the head as far as possible on the left shoulder. Do these exercises in sets of one hundred as many times as one desires.

Start the third exercise by leaning the chin as far as possible down on the chest, then lift the head backward as far as possible. Do these exercises in sets of one hundred as many times as one desires.

Chapter 5

On the morning of the big town hall meeting, Jim-Niacin followed his daily routine of taking care of the citizens of Health-land Kingdom. Jim-Niacin tried to take care of all loose ends concerning the town hall meeting by making a lot of last minute phone calls. He rehearsed the program with his cousin B-12 who would be the moderator for tonight's town hall meeting.

At seven o'clock p.m. sharp Jim-Niacin arrived at the local high school gymnasium, the location of tonight's town hall meeting. The meeting was scheduled to start at eight o'clock p.m. There were several satellite trucks already in place when he arrived. There were the local radio and TV crews as well as reporters from the big super cure all metropolis.

Arriving at the high school was familiar territory for Captain Fredrico. He had walked at the high school track three or more times a week for several years. The high school track was a popular walking place for the citizens of Health-land Kingdom. Captain Fredrico felt that walking or some type of physical fitness program is a must to maintain good health.

It is a fact that one in good physical condition has almost a ten times better chance of surviving a heart attack, stroke, or any ailment. Also, physical activity plays a big role in controlling diabetes. A big help with diabetes is controlling what one eats. Most humans can control diabetes by cutting way back on starches and sweets and taking a chromium picolinate at each meal.

One needs to eat less meat and include more peas, beans, fresh fruits, and raw vegetables. One needs to include at least one raw fruit or vegetable at each meal because cooking and microwaving food destroys all enzymes and most vitamins.

Enzymes are involved in almost every bodily function, especially the digestive process. Enzymes are mostly divided into two groups: digestive enzymes and metabolic enzymes. The digestive enzymes break down food enabling the body to function properly.

The human body manufactures a limited supply of enzymes, but in order to prevent indigestion and other digestive problems one should get as many enzymes as possible from raw food. Otherwise, the body's limited supply becomes depleted.

Jim could see that there was going to be a very big turnout for tonight's event. It seemed like his hard work on getting the word out had paid off. Several tables were set up at one end of the gymnasium to try to accommodate as many as possible on the big panel of vitamins, minerals, humans, herbs, and other nutrients.

Everyone were handed a program as they filed into the gymnasium. It read that, "We will not be able to accommodate everyone due to the time it would take. The moderator will ask all questions, but he will take a few written questions from the audience." At exactly eight p.m. sharp B-12 (vitamin B-12) strode up to the podium.

"Greetings, my fellow vitamins, minerals, humans, herbs, and other nutrients, I'm B-12 your moderator for tonight's town hall meeting," he said. "First I would like to welcome our town's fathers, celebrities, and all other dignitaries to this town hall meeting. Now, I would like to thank the vitamin that made it all happen. He is truly another unsung hero. Many of you here tonight probably have never heard of him, but all of the while he has been out there everyday doing his job. He is one of the lesser known members of the powerful B vitamin family. I am proud to say this truly unsung hero is my first cousin Jim-Niacin (vitamin B-3). Stand up, Jim."

"Thank you, thank you, thank you," said Jim-Niacin as he stood and the audience loudly applauded. "Now," said B-12, "before we get into questions and answers we are going to let several members on our panel down here give their name and vocation. We will start with me. I'm B-12 (vitamin B-12). One of my many jobs is to assure proper digestion and the absorption of food."

"I'm Jane-Ginkgo Biloba. I'm a very well known herb. I'm mostly

Known for improving memory."
"I'm Sammy-Oat Bran Tablets. I'm known for my fiber. Fiber does so many things, for now I will mention just two, I lower the blood cholesterol and help stabilize blood sugar."

"I'm Eddie-calcium. I'm a mineral and I do many things. I'm most needed for strong bones and teeth and to help lower blood pressure."
"I'm Mary-Magnesium. I'm a mineral and of the many things that I do, enzyme activity is most vital. I also assist calcium and potassium uptake."

"I'm Sue-Chromium. I'm a mineral and of the many things that I do, maintaining stable blood sugar levels is most vital."
"I'm VA (vitamin A). I'm a vitamin and lesser known antioxidant. My main job is protecting the eyes and some skin problems."
"I'm Dee Dee (vitamin D). I'm a vitamin, and I'm needed for the absorption of calcium and phosphorus."

Days To USA Economic Collapse 15 November 2017, 1825-0, 1824-0, 1823-0, 1822-0, 1821-0...

"I'm Ned-Zinc. I'm a mineral and of the many things that I do, keeping the prostate gland healthy is most vital."

"I'm Kenny-Saw Pametto. I'm an herb, my main job is to prevent the enlargement of the prostate gland."

"I'm Gina-Evening Primrose Oil. I'm an essential fatty acid. I'm a necessity that cannot be made by the human body. I do many things, but improving the skin is my favorite."

"I'm Patty-Potassium. I'm a mineral. Of my many jobs I will name just a few. I help maintain a healthy nervous system and regulate heart rhythm, also I help control the body's water balance."

"I'm Hannah-Garlic. I'm an herb. I detoxify and protect the body against infections. I help lower blood pressure, aid circulation and perform many other functions."

"I'm Henry-Acidophilus. I'm a

friendly bacteria. My main job is to aid digestion."

"I'm Bonnie-Papaya. I'm an herb. I aid digestion. I'm good for heartburn, indigestion, and bowel disorders."

"I'm Brad-Cranberry Fruit. I'm an herb. I'm helpful for fighting infections of the urinary track."

"I'm Stewart-Ginger Root. I'm an herb. I do many things, but cleaning the colon, reducing spasms, and stomach cramps is my favorite."

"I'm Calvin-Fenugreek. I'm good for the stomach, intestines, eyes, asthma, sinus, inflammation, and lung disorders. I also increase sexual desire."

"I'm Edna-Echinacea. I'm an herb. I have anti viral properties and I help boost the immune system. I'm very helpful against colds and flu."
"I'm Gene-Golden Seal. I'm an herb. I act as an antibiotic, and have

anti-inflammatory and antibacterial properties."

I'm David-Dandelion root. I am an herb. I help cleanse the blood stream and liver and increase the production of bile. I'm used as a diuretic. I help reduce uric acid and improve functioning of the stomach and other vital organs.

"That is the last introduction we will have time for," said B-12. "Now, I will ask the panel a few written questions given to me from the audience, but first let me explain our role here. Number one is we try to be the first line of defense on protecting Health-land Kingdom from Mr. Disease and his cohorts.

"We have some citizens who don't believe in us and won't use our services. The next thing is we don't try to be everything to everybody, our services and abilities are limited.

We encourage anyone that has doubts or don't believe in us to take the super

MD highway to the cure all metropolis. Still, there is a lot we can do to keep Mr. Disease and his friends from gaining a foothold here in Health-land Kingdom.

"Very important: When taking the super MD highway to the cure all metropolis, make sure you tell them which of our services you are maintaining.

"Now, when I ask a question to the panel, please let those that specialize in that particular area of expertise answer the question. Time will not allow me to ask but only a few questions. My first question to the panel is what can we do to combat prostate disease?" he asked.
"I'm Ned-Zinc, and I recommend 50 mg. of zinc per day."

"I'm Larry-Pumpkin Seed Oil, and I recommend 1000 mg. of pumpkin seed oil per day."
"I'm Kenny-Saw Pametto, and I recommend 160 mg. of saw pametto extract twice per day."

Days To USA Economic Collapse 15 November 2017, 1825-0, 1824-0, 1823-0, 1822-0, 1821-0...

"I'm VE (vitamin E), and I recommend 1000 I.U. of vitamin E per day."

"I'm Jim-Niacin, and I recommend my maintenance dose of 250 mg. of niacin per day."

"Is there anyone else?" said B-12. "So, that gives us five weapons to fight prostate disease, and I'm pretty darn sure that anyone that arms themselves with these weapons will be able to keep Mr. prostate disease away for a very long time, if not forever. My next question to the panel is what can we do to deal with diabetes disease?"

"I'm Sue-Chromium, and I recommend 200 mg. of chromium picolinate three times a day at meal time. I also would like to elaborate a little on this terrible disease.

"Diet plays a major role in controlling this terrible disease. Everyone with this disease should be able to home check his blood sugar level and keep it under control. But, controlling blood sugar is not the only problem diabetics face.

"There are problems with the eyes, blood circulation, and many others. There is a problem with nerve damage (neuropathy) especially in the lower extremities," she concluded.

"I'm VE (vitamin E), and I recommend 1000 I.U. of vitamin E per day. Being a natural blood thinner makes me a great asset to a diabetic."

"I'm Jim-Niacin, and I recommend my maintenance dose of 250 mg. of niacin once per day for one not showing any diabetic symptoms. On the other hand, for anyone experiencing the symptoms of diabetes, especially numbness in the lower extremities I recommend my unclogging dose of 250 mg. of niacin twice per day.

"Too high of a dose of niacin can cause liver damage and high blood sugar levels, but too low of a dose does no good. The 500 mg.

maximum dose per day seems to be just enough to be effective.

"There have been many lower extremities cut off because of diabetes, but I truly believe that if they had only given Jim-Niacin a chance I would have saved some of those limbs."

"Is there anyone else?" said B-12. "There it is folks, three powerful weapons to deal with this scourge diabetes. Now, for the final question of the evening, the question is what can we do to prevent extremely dry skin?"

"I'm Gina-Evening Primrose Oil, I'm an essential fatty acid and I'm one of the good oils that the body needs for beautiful skin. I recommend 1000-3000 mg. of evening primrose oil per day."

"I'm Jim-Niacin. In my view problems with dry skin, toe nail funguses, dandruff, and other skin problems is almost always a problem with blood circulation especially in the capillaries and small blood vessels.

"For extremely dry skin I recommend my unclogging dose of 250 mg. twice per day after a meal until the extremely dry skin condition has been cured, then throttle down to 250 mg. once a day for maintenance. But, be aware, most humans fear me, and for good reason, because my doses are no Sunday picnic or stroll through the park. My doses may heat up your skin like it is on fire and turn it as red as a beet.

"This flushing process is unpredictable, sometimes it will not happen at all, then other times it will last anywhere from five minutes to thirty minutes. It may not be pleasant, but it is my only way of unclogging the capillaries and small blood vessels," said Jim-Niacin.

"Is there anyone else?" said B-12. "What more could one ask for; those were two of the most powerful remedies that I ever heard of in

Days To USA Economic Collapse 15 November 2017, 1825-0, 1824-0, 1823-0, 1822-0, 1821-0...

dealing with a pesky humiliating dry skin condition.

"Remember, a dry skin problem is not something to be taken lightly, because you can see what is happening to the outer skin, but what's taking place inside with the vital organs could be a lot worse. "Citizens of Health-land Kingdom, that will end our town hall meeting for tonight, I would like to thank everyone for coming. Have a safe drive home," he said.

Chapter 6

Captain Fredrico was very impressed with the town hall meeting, especially learning how to deal with his long time dry skin problem and toe nail fungus. It had got to the point that he hated to take a shower.

It was bad enough struggling

through the warmer months of the year, but the approach of winter was almost terrifying because a dry skin problem becomes much worse during the winter months. Much of the time during the winter he had to resort to what is called a bird bath by washing only his arm pits and private area. He had tried all kinds of oils, both internal and external. He had traveled on the super MD highway to the cure all metropolis, but all to no avail. Since the town hall meeting he had started off on Jim-Niacin's unclogging dose of 250 mg. of niacin twice a day after a meal.

The resulting benefits were obvious within a couple of days. Within days the treatment was so effective that the captain could barely wait to jump into the shower for the slightest reason. Also, within days his toe nails had started clearing and should be completely clear within a few months.

Also, in a few months the mayoral election will be taking place.

Days To USA Economic Collapse 15 November 2017, 1825-0, 1824-0, 1823-0, 1822-0, 1821-0...

Captain Fredrico felt very good about his chances of winning. According to the latest poll he had a four point lead.

That night as he and Jan were setting in the den watching TV, Captain Fredrico said, "You know, Jan, if I do become mayor of Healthland Kingdom I'm going to recognize Jim-Niacin by declaring a Jim-Niacin day."

"I know, dear, how much you love Jim-Niacin. He made it possible for you to be able to take regular showers again without you having to lotion down almost your whole body."
"I don't care how much he is feared and misunderstood," said the Captain. "As far as I'm concerned Jim-Niacin is a miracle vitamin."

"I agree, my darling husband, about Jim-Niacin's abilities, if humans would just give him a chance he would save most of the lower extremities that are being lost because of Mr. Diabetes Disease."

The Captain got up from his recliner, walked over to Jan and gave her a warm tender kiss on her waiting luscious lips and said, "I'm off to bed, dear, I'll wait up for you."
"I won't be long, dear," said Jan.

      Things had been rather calm in Health-land Kingdom for the last few months VC, VE, and John-pyridoxine all were very busy taking care of the town's population. About the only thing going on was the mayoral election coming up very soon.

They all thought the town hall meeting did a lot of good for the community. They felt it educated the citizens that there was a lot they could do for themselves concerning their health care.

That means that one will not have to jump on the super MD highway for the slightest little pin prick or minor inconvenience. Sure, there

is only so much we vitamins, minerals, herbs, etc. can do to promote health, we don't try to be everything to everybody.
After the town hall meeting Mr.

Disease was steaming mad. He was even thinking of calling a meeting of all the different diseases. The nerve of those vitamins, minerals, humans, herbs and other nutrients trying to get together and put him and his friends out of business.

They want to try to put his most successful friends like cancer, diabetes, heart disease, and AIDS out of business. He was not having it; that was not going to be tolerated. Mr. Disease started planning.

He would try to attack their left flank by bringing back some of his old friends like the Black Plague, Tuberculosis, and West Nile, next he would try to rush their right flank with AIDS to try to split their force, then he would try to rout them up the middle with lots of Cancer and Heart Disease.

I will take no prisoners. Who do they think this is, this is Mr. Disease and I don't play, I even quit school because they had recess. It is on. How dare they have this town hall meeting to try and get rid of me and my friends.

After a long hot summer the day of the mayoral election had finally arrived and it looked like it was going to be a big turn out. At seven o'clock p.m. Captain Fredrico, Jan, Bob, and Melinda had comfortable seats at election headquarters. All of the election precincts closed at seven o'clock p.m. sharp.

The captain and his family started watching the tally on the big electronic board as the precincts came in. Captain Fredrico jumped out to an early four point lead and

Days To USA Economic Collapse 15 November 2017, 1825-0, 1824-0, 1823-0, 1822-0, 1821-0...

was able to maintain the lead throughout the night as the precincts came in. Then, finally the election supervisor announced, "Citizens of Health-land Kingdom the mayor elect is Orry Fredrico." Within seconds several microphones were thrust in Captain Fredrico's face.

A reporter was almost yelling, "Captain Fredrico, how does it feel being the mayor elect of Health-land Kingdom."

"First, I would like to thank my family and all of the volunteers that worked so hard on my behalf to make this happen. Next, I would like to thank all of the citizens of Health-land Kingdom who had the faith and trust in me and backed it up by turning out to vote for me.

"Also, I would like to inform those that did not vote for me that I will be mayor of all the citizens of Health-land Kingdom. Finally, I would like to thank my opponent for a good clean hard fought campaign. Thanks again everyone. Good night."

Chapter 7

About one month after Captain Fredrico had been sworn in as mayor of Health-land Kingdom, he announced that the first Saturday in March would be recognized by the town as Jim-Niacin's day.

On the morning of the first Saturday in March Mayor Fredrico stood at the podium at Healthy living park before a very large crowd.

"Citizens of Health-land Kingdom, today as your mayor I am proclaiming today as Jim-Niacin's day. We have on hand plenty of free food, drinks, and entertainment. To kick off this festive day, I'm going to deliver this short speech about the vitamin citizen we are celebrating

Days To USA Economic Collapse 15 November 2017, 1825-0, 1824-0, 1823-0, 1822-0, 1821-0... today.

"Citizens of Health-land, Jim-Niacin is sort of an enigma. Many here had never heard of him, and of those that had, many of them fear and hate him. Still there is a great many that love this vitamin to death.

"I myself am one of those that dearly love Jim-Niacin and the good work he does. I am not telling you what I heard about Jim-Niacin, I'm telling you what I've personally experienced with my dealing with Jim-Niacin. I'm giving it to you first hand, straight from the horse's mouth.

"As I've told my wife and many others, I don't care what anyone says, to me Jim-Niacin is a miracle vitamin. This small, quiet, lowly member of the powerful B vitamin family is a Godsend as far as I'm concerned. As a proud virile human male I think of the many, many years that I suffered with extremely dry skin.

"For years I tried everything to get relief from this annoying dry skin condition. Even at the cure all metropolis they just prescribed an extremely expensive body cream that did little better than cheap over-the-counter lotions.

"Bathing and warm water had become the enemy. Washing only arm pits and the private area was becoming the norm, and I just hated my predicament. To me cleanliness is next to Godliness.

"Sure, I had heard of Jim-Niacin, but it was mainly bad stuff, I never knew about his real power until I attended the town hall meeting. Over the years the dry skin problem was getting worse. Some type of fungus had invaded my toe nails and my skin was losing its luster in a few locations.

"The battle for healthy skin was a battle I knew I was losing , but no one could help me and I didn't know what to do. All of my life I've never been a

Days To USA Economic Collapse 15 November 2017, 1825-0, 1824-0, 1823-0, 1822-0, 1821-0...

quitter, I knew there was an answer, the problem was finding it, so I just kept on searching and searching.

"I was at my wits end, nothing or no one seemed able to help me find relief from my extremely dry skin condition. Then, at the final hour when all seemed lost and there was no hope left, Jim-Niacin came riding in on a big white horse at the town hall meeting.

"At the town hall meeting Jim-Niacin gave out his unclogging dose of 250 mg. twice a day after a meal. The first thing is I must warn you that taking Jim-Niacin's unclogging dose is no cake walk or stroll through the park. That is the reason many who have tried taking Jim's doses don't like him and is afraid of him.

"When Jim goes to work unclogging those capillaries and small blood vessels it is not pleasant by any means. This flushing process varies in intensity, sometimes it may be mild, then at other times your skin may feel like it is literally on fire.

"This flushing process may last anywhere from five to thirty minutes, but seldom lasts more than thirty minutes. I have no evidence to support this, but I believe diabetes itself is caused by a deficiency in niacin, chromium, and a few other nutrients.

"Citizens of Health-land I could go on and on praising Jim-Niacin because in the past he truly has been an unsung hero. I will add this and come to a close. Don't ever go over his maximum 500 mg. daily dose or it could cause liver damage.

"In closing, I will assure you that his unclogging dose got rid of my dandruff, dry skin, toe nail fungus, etc. Stand up Jim-Niacin and say a few words," concluded Captain Fredrico.

As Jim-Niacin arrived at the podium he stood tall and proud. The audience went wild with

Days To USA Economic Collapse 15 November 2017, 1825-0, 1824-0, 1823-0, 1822-0, 1821-0...

applause, then chanted, "We love you Jim, we love you Jim, we love you "Thank you, thank you, thank you," said Jim-Niacin, "and may God bless this great town and keep it healthy always."

THE END

FREDDIE LEE SIRMANS SENIOR WEBSITE: www.FLSirmans.com

www.ingramcontent.com/pod-product-compliance
Lightning Source LLC
Chambersburg PA
CBHW071200240526
45470CB00017B/663